Brother

Elliott Hudson

Published by Elliott Hudson

Exterior design by Haley Maddock
Printed in the United States of America
Non-fiction

PUBLISHER'S NOTE

Certain names, places, and words have been replaced with … in this text to protect the privacy of the mentioned. However, the names of family members of the author and the name of Mr. Curt Stewart have been kept in. Every word in this text is from the original journal of Elliott Hudson. To protect the truth and maintain the integrity of the original document, this book contains everything written, from front to back, exactly as it appears in the original journal. Because it was originally written as a personal journal, it is understood and accepted that there are English and grammatical errors all throughout the work. But, truth was the main goal in publishing this work, so nothing was edited. This work is being published out of care and love. The goal of the book is strictly to help people who wish to seek its reason. The people and things written about inside have all paid a huge sacrifice to be included. They must be completely respected and in no way downgraded or hassled because of any content in this book. The author's family has been through an extraordinary amount of pain, and this book is not a notion against them, but rather a testament to their remarkable strength, miraculous courage and unprecedented love. In no way, shape or form is the work herein intended to insult, offend or damage anyone or anything in any way. Its only purpose is to teach and provide insight into powerful and important subject matter. Remember, there would be no good, if there was no bad. It is your decision whether you choose to read beyond this page or not. Enjoy.

ISBN-13: 978-1477657805

Foreword

I first met Elliott in early February of 2012. At that time, I was going through some of the darkest days of my life. I was suffering from a long-term, crippling depression, I had just lost my job for the umpteenth time, and I had generally given up on life. After having discovered my plans to take my own life after getting my house in order, a very good friend of mine had recommended that I seek inpatient professional care, and that I do so immediately. I have always been of the opinion that group therapy, and inpatient care in particular, was not for me. Though long-suffering with severe bipolar disorder, I thought that these types of therapies were for people with much more severe cases than mine. I've always had a powerful ability to diminish the level of my own mental illness, as I'm sure most people suffering from bipolar do. After much debate and convincing on her part (bless her), my friend was able to convince me to check in to an inpatient facility in Newburgh, Indiana. On my very first night, I decided that all of my fears and suspicions had been confirmed, and this place was not for me. The noise of the nightshift workers, the regulated smoking breaks, and the general lack of freedom all convinced me to seek an immediate release. Thankfully, like most facilities of this type, the staff required a 24-hour observation period before allowing the release of an admitted patient. It was in these 24 hours where things began to change for me.

I attended my first group therapy session

the morning of my first day. I will say that, despite the first session confirming my fears of the ineffectiveness of group therapy, in retrospect, the therapy session itself was completely derailed by none other than yours truly. Because of my arrogance, I was unable to see the process for what it was: the relating of similar stories by people who were suffering just as much as I was. Because it was my nature at the time, I did nothing save try to find fault in every detail of the therapist's words. The meeting eventually degenerated into nothing more than a semantic argument between the therapist and me. As a result, this first session, I was unable to hear the stories of those that were on this journey with me, and I left feeling more downtrodden than ever. It was after this session that the therapist pulled me aside and had a one-on-one discussion with me about the purpose and path of group therapy. She showed me a new way to look at the group, and I decided that I would give it one more try during the afternoon session.

In the interim, I decided that I would spend my time getting to know the people around me. If I was to be stuck in this place for another day, I might as well enjoy the company. It was at this time that I met and began my friendship with Elliott. At first, it was simply a casual getting-to-know-you session, and I found him to be an intelligent, funny, and intriguing young man. It confused me why one so full of promise—young, a good student, a talented athlete, and great plans for the future—was in this facility with someone like me. His friendship alone, however, was enough to get me through the day.

When the afternoon therapy session rolled around, I decided to take the advice of the therapist and let others tell their stories and vent their frustrations. I could not have made a better decision. It was at this time that I truly realized that I was not alone. There were others in the world who were suffering from various mental illnesses and past traumas that not only equaled, but sometimes dwarfed, my own. And then came Elliott's story. By this time, Elliott had already developed a positive mental outlook, despite all that he had been through. To hear his story was nothing short of inspirational. Though young, Elliott had suffered through so much in his short time here on earth, yet he had learned from those experiences and had decided to use them to help those around him. As I sat and listened to what he struggled with prior to being admitted, and what he was still struggling with at that time, I was struck by the power of his attitude to change his own circumstances and make life worth living. I was so moved by his words that—after the session was over—I felt compelled to approach him and tell him what a difference he had made. Though half my age, this young man had shown me the start of my path to mental wellness. He was truly an inspiration to me, and I told him so.

Over the coming days, Elliott and I developed a very powerful bond. We shared stories of our lives and the pain we had dealt with throughout. We cried together, and we laughed together. During these times, Elliott would share with me bits and pieces of the journal you are about to read. Some of the most powerful epiphanies I had during my time at the facility were as a direct result of these readings. Not only does he have insight well beyond his years, but also Elliott was able to couch that insight into language that spoke to me, and language I knew then would speak to others. I'm glad that I was able to help encourage him to share his story with the rest of the world.

Though I eventually had to check out of the facility and begin my life anew, I will always cherish the time that I spent there and the amazing life lessons I've learned. Though we are miles apart, I am thankful that I was able to take both Elliott's friendship and his words of inspiration with me on my new journey. I hope you will find in them the wisdom that helped me get through my darkest days.

Curt Stewart

Brother

January 10

Every day is a battle. Every moment. Every second. I've learned- so much in my battle. My battle rips me to pieces. It makes me weak. But I get stronger. I've been fighting this battle since the night of December 4, 2011. I will never forget. Hours, minutes, seconds from dying. From killing myself. Little did I know the thoughts wouldn't go away. I am a slave to my own mind. So today, January 10, I start my journal. I love writing, and my therapist wants me to write down my thoughts. I don't know if I'll show her or not. I have been needing someone to talk to anyways, so you can be the brother I've always wanted.

January 11

Sticking with this for at least a day now. They think I might have mono. Sucks ass. Can't get back in a normal routine because I keep fucking getting sick. Why can I not catch a break? Why will nothing fucking go my way? Huh? Bullshit. I go through hell every day and get nothing back? But this fucking life? That I fucking hate? I don't want the future. I don't want tomorrow. I hate today. Fuck school. Fuck sports. Fuck expectations. Fuck the future. Fuck my life. Fuck these thoughts that won't leave. Dammit. I'm shaking again. What a fucking surprise. My breathing speeds up. I progressively become more pissed off. My breath is loud. I want to hurt myself. The thoughts stream through my head. They won't stop. Fuck this. Fuck them.

I'm forced to suffer through these times. I call them break downs. It is hard to write I am shaking so bad. I don't want to fucking live. Yes I do. Stay strong. Fuck this. No one deserves this. Why am I here? Death is so pretty, so welcoming. Help me God and Jesus. Help. I have no one else. Breathe. Relax. I know it's hard. Breathe. I hate it. Help. Please. Help. I can't control my thoughts. I need to step away. Blurry. Shaky. Attacks. I can't breathe. Dizzy. My body is tingling. My therapist calls these meltdowns. I can see her. I can't think. Help. Why am I different? Sweating. Why me? Look me in the fucking eyes and tell me. What are you? Where did you come from? I've got something to say to you. FUCK YOU MOTHER FUCKER. You want to fuck with me? Cut me. Stomach. I've done it before. Not scared. Wrist. Face. Leg. Temple. Heart. Stab. Please. End it. I can't hold still. I want to put a fucking hole in the wall with my fist. Fuck you. I can't read right. Where are you? I see you in my mind. Circling. Laughing. Torture. Torture. Pen. Do you ever cry? Have you ever wanted death? Fucking tell me you fuck! God will beat you. God will win. Suck it pussy. You don't know me. Fuck you. White powder. Not good. Be strong. Overcome. Hold me. Stay with me. I know who I am. Maybe. I hope.

What the fuck am I doing? I have fucking mono or some shit so I'm just sitting here alone all day. Hitting up twitter like a damn boss. Fucking thoughts won't stop though. Pissing me off. Now I'll have to go back to school and have no fucking clue what's going on. Fuck school. Fuck make up work. Fucking counselor put me in three college classes. Are you shitting me? I don't give a fuck about school. I don't do shit or give a fuck. I fucking hate this. My future near and far is a big bag of shit. I'd rather be dead.

No one understands me here. No one gives a shit. I'd rather be in a fucking hospital. I'd rather live there. No fucking problems in there. Don't have to deal with this dumb ass town and its dumb ass people there. I wanted to stay in the hospital the last time. A million times better than my damn life. Expectations from everyone are controlling my life. Teachers, parents, coaches, girls, friends, everyone fucking expects everything from me. I'll tell you what, do something once, and people will expect it from you every time after. Ocd made me a perfect little fuck before so now I'm just expected to be perfect all the time and I fucking hate it. Anything less and I'm looked down on. Fuck that. The more you do something, the more people will expect it of you. So be yourself. Always. Before you get shaped into something you're not. What do you want people to expect of you? I already ruined my damn life. I'm never happy. I never want to do anything except lay and rot. I have nothing to look forward to. I'm in a world I don't want to be in and there is no way out. I hate life. No one fucking knows what I go through every damn second. Fuck expectations. I'm done with this shit. I don't want to go back. People just fucking stare at me and don't understand my problems. They don't know what's going on. They just look at me in disgust. I just want to lay here and die. No more problems. No more worries. I wish I could just be in Heaven. They're lucky. They're all lucky. The people who don't understand. I used to be one. Everyone who doesn't understand why anyone would ever want to kill them self is lucky. Because once you think about it once, it doesn't go away. Once you consider it once, it doesn't go away. And once you want to once, it never goes away. It's always sitting there in the back of your mind. The ultimate solution. The ultimate answer. The ultimate ending. Just die and everything will go away. Just die Elliott. Do it. It eats at me every second. Just die. Just do it.

The white powder calls me. It begs me to come back. It tells me I need it. That I can't move on without it. I want it. It takes me to a different world. I lose my senses. My ears scream the ring loudly. It's all I hear. Ring. Intense, very intense, blaring ringing. I see myself from above. Like a dream. Alive down there, but I'm up here. The world I see around me isn't the logical world we live in. My skin, my whole body is tingling. Almost numb. I am not aware of what is going on around me. I can not control my mind. I can not think for myself. This world is different. The things around me blend together into a blurry daze. I become cold and scared. I can not function for myself. This white powder is different than anything I've ever done. Weed and alcohol don't compare. I leave my body with this drug. I use way more than I'm supposed to. I already take controlled substances for my anxiety, depression and ocd. I try to walk, but I collapse. My body lies crippled on the ground. Hours go by. Shaking. I can't move. I'm incapable of performing any type of action. My body is paralyzed by my mind. All of my senses are tingling and buzzing. I close my eyes, quiet my mind and let the drug take me over. Peace. Calm. Relaxed. I let it do its thing. I become friends with it. We like each other. I smile. The drug and I become powerful as one. I am drifting through a different land. Life is perfect in the moment. I fall asleep in peace. For once. I smoke the white powder for two days. Reality becomes different. The drug and I keep growing together. We become more happy and connected. I embrace it the second night. Life is good. But the day after I can't use anymore. I must go home. I'm forced back into normal life. My body feels empty. I begin shaking. I break down worse than ever. I need the drug. During my breakdowns it is now the drug that tortures me. My mind becomes transfixed with memories of the drug and thoughts of death. I scream. Ache. Moan. The thoughts torture my soul, my heart, my mind. I weep. I become dizzy. My screams become so violent they turn silent. My mom and step-dad watch as I lie crippled once more. It is the hardest battle I've ever had to fight. Every second and every thought rip my heart and soul to shreds. Why do I live like this? Thoughts of suicide race through my mind in an infinite circle. I take the pain. It gives me what I deserve. I think I am crazy. I claw and thrash in my bed. At its peak I imagine a knife. Slicing my throat. Penetrating my heart. It is so strong it takes over completely. I become incapable of fighting back. I let the pain soak through me like I let the drug. It tortures me with every amount of power it has. It consumes every inch of me into its wrath. Into its pain. Depression sets in so I lay there for hours. It happens again the next day. On the third day, the pain of the drug starts to lessen. As more days go by I need it less and less until it barely crosses my mind. Until now. Now as I sit here alone and with nothing, it has come back. It itches at me again. They told me it was synthetic marijuana, but I don't know what it really was. I do know how to get it. I'll have a chance tomorrow if I want, but I don't know what I want. I don't know where I'm going. I don't know what to do.

January 12

I am so sad. So weak. So vulnerable. I hate myself. Everything I worked so hard for is gone. I'm scared. Scared of myself and scared of the future. I don't even want to lie here anymore. I'm so hopeless. There's nothing for me here. I just count the seconds. I'm tired, but I can't sleep. I've completely let myself go. I don't care anymore. Absolutely no motivation. I just lie in bed for days and weeks at a time. None of my dreams came true. I tried harder than anyone else. If one fucking thing would have gone right I would have been fine. I am completely lost.

I'm not getting up. I'll probably just pee the bed. I'm so worthless. I swear if my mom brings schoolwork home for me I'm not fucking doing it. This is the shittiest feeling ever. I'm immobilized on my bed in a state of confusion and hate. Suicide just keeps circling around my mind. Weighing the reasons to do it against the reasons not to. The not to's are disappearing. Maybe only one left, I don't want to go to hell. Because that's even worse than this. I can't even imagine having to feel worse than this. FOREVER. Never-ending time feeling worse than this? Now that is hell. I'm really hoping I don't have anymore breakdowns. Then I can't think for myself. I'm scared of what I'll do. I wonder if my time here is short. I have nothing to live for anyways, but everything to die for. I'm thinking about starting a suicide note. I think about death all day and night. I know there are going to be more breakdowns. What am I going to do?

FUCKING BULLSHIT! What a great fucking day! My fucking girlfriend broke up with me after two and a half years. We were supposed to get fucking married! Fuck girls! Fuck everyone! The only thing all you mother fuckers care about is yourselves. I HATE MY FUCKING LIFE! IU fucking lost tonight. Bullshit! I have absolutely nothing. Fuck! I want to fucking die! The knife is on my chest. My heart. I'm going to fucking do it! It's over! Why am I here!? This is fucking bullshit! Am I not good enough for you!? I am beating the shit out of everything because I hate fucking everything! Do you understand!? I belong in a fucking hospital! You don't fucking know me! I will kill you! I don't fucking care anymore! If you lived in my life for one fucking day you would go fucking crazy! Am I not good enough for you!? I wasn't for her! Fuck you! Fuck this! I'm gonna do it! This is rock bottom like never before. This feeling is killing me and I'm bawling and I can't stop. Don't fucking judge me you inconsiderate prick. Knife in my heart pleaseee. I will push you. It would feel soooo good. No one knows what I fucking go through! My mind is exploding! It is torture. AAAAAAAHHHHHHHHH!!!!!!!!!!!!!!! Kill me now you fucking bastard! Kill me! I have no one! Cry! Cry you bastard! Have you ever wanted to die? What are you!? What have you done with me!? Please. Please. Please. Something go right. They don't understand. You have no heart! Get out of my mind! You don't even care do you!? Dammit. Eat fucking shit. Lick it off the fucking ground. I. AM. NOT. CRAZY. Fucking believe me you bastard. I fucking hate everything! So fucking hate me back! I'm ready for it to stop. I'm ready. I'm ready. I'm ready! Die! Knife. Is this fucking good enough dammit!? Have you gotten what you want? You don't know how much you have. So you just sit and laugh, and I'll just suffer. Awesome! You fucking listen to me. Listen you fucker. I know you don't care. I know it'll all just pass through your head. But listen. Listen to my feelings and see how you feel. Hostile trapped desperate hurt useless rejected dead unappreciated backstabbed fucked up fucked over weak done giving up not my fault you don't even come close to understanding none no one no one does no one cares provoked defeated ignored frantic hate outrage panic misery is that good enough for you are you sorry do you have a heart of course you don't confusion anger devastation fury I can't control it guilt horrified no hope no worth why can't I just be dead my heart is melting are you perfect I hope you appreciate what you stand for don't act like you know me there is nothing left I am empty I want to kill me sooooo bad it is torture but you don't care is this entertaining fuck you feel some emotion like I have to every second cry cry cry please cry with me are you scared I'm not fuck you die fucking die humiliated insecure alone I hope you're happy I want to use the knife so bad I'm done with this. Fuuuccccckkkkk youuuuuuuuuuu. Death. I see you.

I wish you could feel endless pain. I wish you could feel endless hunger. I wish you could watch me wither. Watch me scream. Watch me rip my hair out. I wish you burst into tears every time you stared into the mirror. When's the last time you wanted one of your kids to die? Huh? Yeah, feel for my parents. Am I a selfish bastard? You think I'm selfish because I say that? Okay, that's fair, let's trade lives then. No. You'd crumble in a heartbeat. You'd go back to your normal self so haunted that you'd roll up into a ball in a little dark corner somewhere and never come out until a little boy found your unidentifiable pile of bones and used them to win the next science fair. Yeah, what you don't understand is what rock bottom really is. I mean really, really is. So don't even begin to judge me. Don't even begin to try to imagine it. You can only understand it if it happens to you. My heart hurts so bad. It's rotting into a dry, black raisin. It's not worth it. Do you remember the last time you hurt so bad you wept for hours? Do you remember that pain? What was it about? Imagine that feeling all the time. Never a glimpse of light to give you hope. Never a breath of fresh air. My heart feels dead.

He used to touch me when he thought I was asleep. Rub my nipples. Play with my penis. Lick his fingers and stroke it. See how far up my butt he could get his finger. I never said a word. I never reacted. I was too small, too scared to do anything about it. I just let him. I took it. I'll never tell who it was. I couldn't do that to him. It wasn't my parents of course, but still, it haunts me. I don't know what to think.

January 13

Sitting in fucking school today. I hate this shitty place, and I just got here. Right off the bat my first teacher makes a rude ass comment about me not being here lately. I wish he fucking knew. Thinking about just walking out ... Another fucking comment. Been in here for ten damn minutes. Don't know what to do. Pissed off ... Thoughts about kicking his ass are starting to look really nice ... This is hell. Every single second, every single thought I have is contemplating suicide. I hate my life. I hate this ... People just sit around and ask me what's wrong. YOU DON'T FUCKING UNDERSTAND. JUST SHUT THE HELL UP, LIVE YOUR LIFE, AND LEAVE ME THE FUCK ALONE … Thank you … …. You're awesome. You aren't like the others. You know about the world like I do. Thank you.

Okay, so some girls have great personalities, some girls do not. Some girls are hott, some girls are not. You've got to find the perfect balance between the two if you want the right girl, and right now I just can't seem to get it right. Now there is this one girl I met at the hospital, and we've kept in touch since. I'm starting to like her. But she lives an hour away. The other girl I care about, and she really likes me, we talk a lot, about everything if you know what I mean, is a …. Oh shit.

I had to sit and watch my team play again tonight without me. One of my best friends got hurt. I really cared for him, but he can't remember. So. Like always. No breaks, all depression for me. Isn't life great!? I'm surprised I'm still here. Probably going back to the hospital soon. I really, really hope I don't get sent to the adult unit.

January 15

I've had a pretty fucked up weekend. Last night I took my first dip. Didn't throw up. Sat me on my ass big time though. Smoked some delicious weed. Water bong. Dazed a good hour and a half. Got drunk. Beer and mixed drinks. Got a little crazy. Then relaxed and chain smoked some cigs for a while. Best night I've had possibly my whole senior year. But it's only because I know I'm going back to the hospital tomorrow. I also found out what the white powder was. Crack. Synthetic weed huh? People fucking lying about what they give you. No wonder kids get so fucked up these days. Sat around in a circle with my friends last night and got to vent to them. I'm going to hate leaving them again, but I'm too fucked up to stay. I think I changed their lives yesterday when I talked to them. I even cried in front of them. I've had a lot of anxiety about telling my parents and doctors I need to go back. I have trouble disappointing. I have no feeling in my body anymore. Everything just comes and goes. Drugs are my only release from the depression. It's constant. I looked the devil in the eyes last night. Talk about scary shit. Have that happen to you and tell me if anything on Earth ever scares you again. I want to die. I don't know what I'm doing or what to do. People keep talking about me, and I hear about it, and I get really pissed off. I have no control over my actions anymore. I almost t-boned someone in my car last night because I was driving more reckless and stupid than ever. ... ... 's been texting me today. Wants me back. Don't know what to do because of course I can't think straight. I do stupid shit all the time now. Rock bottom is fucking shit. The sex is nice. She's nice. She's pretty. But for some reason I just want to party my life away and fuck everyone I can. I last forever dammit get in the bed this is high school not some long term relationship shit be a slut like every guy wants you to be. I did promise her I'd go talk to her later in person. Here come the tears. Great. I hate seeing her like that. And a hott ... wants to fuck me. Said something about a full body massage Friday night. Gave me her address. Tells me how much she feels for me and wants my cock. All my friends are so jealous it's awesome. She wants to wait but I don't! I don't know how long I'm going to be here! I'm trying to butter her up though. It's working really well. I daydream about doing it. I don't even know if I can cum yet on this new medicine. Couldn't on the last one. Maybe I should just be a porn star.

Whatever. So damn depressed. Hating life. Need drugs. That has been the only thing working. IU plays soon. Better fucking wake their asses up before I start breaking shit.

January 16

My parents have given up on me. It's the last thing I ever expected. They constantly glare at me. They hate me. It's the most painful feeling I have ever felt. I have never been so alone. I feel so empty. They took my phone, my car, my computer, everything. I no longer leave their sight. They look for things to make me do now just for the hell of it. They are so disappointed. It's like they just expected me to come home, get better all of a sudden, and act as if nothing ever happened. I'm scared of Keith. I've never been more depressed. I've never had such realistic thoughts of killing myself. They told me there is nothing for me. They wish I wasn't here. My whole life is gone now. If I can find that I will go to Heaven even if I put the knife in my chest then I will do it. I'm ready to end it. I have no more good feelings left. Nothing. I will kill myself if God and Jesus will forgive me for it. I almost don't even care about that. I can't wait for everything to be over with. I'm scared Keith is going to hurt me. I'm craving drugs. Cigarettes. Alcohol. I love smoking, I don't care what it is. That feeling on your throat, your lungs, then your mind. Beautiful. It's relief. I'm craving. If I'm going to have to be here, I need that shit.

January 17

I hate getting treated like a child. Keith is reading through all my text messages. I'm going cold turkey off all my medication because it's obviously not working. I already feel weak, and I'm completely out of energy and strength. I think I'm going to pass out. I'm shaking again.

I got my schedule changed to just half days so I can still graduate with honors and try to put my life back together at the same time. Definitely not giving anymore effort in high school. I'm so burnt out it's not even funny. I'm so ready for college. I got accepted to IU in September. Good thing I already have 46 credits and a 3.97 GPA to carry me through the rest of this crap.

My parents won't let me just go half days. I'm pissed off and craving drugs again. I seem to only want to use when I get down. The … that has the hotts for me cried today when I went and saw her. I'm starting to see how alike we are. She has problems similar to mine. We are actually starting to get close. I don't know what to do. There might be some love involved. But I believe love and marriage is just chance. There are probably thousands of people in the world each of us could fall in love with and marry. On the other hand, I'm getting pretty pissed off that I can't talk to anybody since I don't have a phone, computer or car. It makes me even more alone. I try to make my parents feel bad about taking them. Today I stepped back into the place where I lived the crack life for two days. Haunting memories. It was terrifying to be back in there. It felt like the room was closing in on me, and it kept getting darker and darker. I had to leave the room it was so horrifying. Then all my memories started to come back from before I started journaling. I thought about when I had searched the house for a razor blade or pocket knife. Then when I couldn't find either, I just grabbed a kitchen knife. I remember cutting my stomach up into six bloody square pieces. On Christmas. I remember doing it even worse the next night. I'm tired of hiding the wounds. I want to show my scars. Then I thought about when I ran away from home. When my mind was unstable, one night after getting back from the hospital, I got into it with my mom over something little. I ended up just packing my bags and leaving. Just walking down the street in the freezing rain. I left my bawling mother and sister crippled in pain at my feet. I remember Keith shouting at me and wanting to fight. I remember shattering both my stress balls off the wall in rage. How could I let my sister see all this? I'm kind of glad I haven't ended up going back to the hospital. At least I'm doing a little better. I saw my therapist and psychiatrist today. I'm still lost. Lost forever. I still can't sleep at night, but I refuse to take the sleeping pills. I still ponder going back to the drug life. I even jokingly asked the ... if she would do some lines with me. She really is great. She's smoking hot, great body, wants me and cares! So what the hell am I doing!? However my parents don't trust me, and I don't want to lie to them again. Tomorrow is just another day brother. Just one after the other.

P.S. - I already feel like I know more than my therapist. She's kind of starting to annoy me. I wonder ... is everything some of these people know just what they've learned from textbooks? Have they ever even experienced any of this before? I could already be more helpful to people than what they are. I know this world.

January 19

There isn't much to say brother. I've lost everyone and everything I had. Tonight I came home to the most hateful parents I've ever experienced. Keith yelled at me and walked out, followed by my mom. Right when I had walked in with a smile on my face I received heart stopping glares. All I did was go play basketball with my friends. Something they had recommended me to do. I had even told Keith exactly where I was going, and he hadn't objected. They don't want me anymore. I haven't even talked to my dad in over a week because they took my phone away. They talk shit about him in front of me, and it makes me furious. I have absolutely nothing. Goodbye brother. I am going to kill myself. Tonight. Toodaloo muthafuckers!

January 21

Dammit. I should be dead. I fucking fell asleep before everyone went to bed the other night so I couldn't over-dose like I wanted to. My parents are fucking bullshit. I lose my car, phone and computer just for sleeping at my friend's house, and I still haven't gotten anything back. And I have to be home every single night. I'M EIGHTFUCKINGTEEN. Now on my Sunday tomorrow they are putting me to work. Yeah right. I'm done! Hey parents! DON'T LOCK YOUR KIDS UP LIKE A FUCKING PRISON BECAUSE IT WILL ONLY END IN FUCKING

SHIT. Tonight I'm going to take every pill I can find and get fucked up beyond belief so I can die right, with Clonapin and Ativan, my only real friends. Then I'm going to carve the shit out of my chest if I can still function. A cross. I don't have long. Your attempt to make me better only made me worse Terry Keith Doug. GOODBYE!

January 22

I guess I have some explaining to do as to why this is being written. Last night I snuck into my parents' room and found where my mom had my best pills hidden. I poured them all into my pockets and hid them in my room. When I was lying in bed plotting how I was going to do it, my mom came in and talked to me. She said she was proud of how I've been doing, and I would start getting things back tomorrow. When she left I started re-thinking what I was about to do. I kept telling myself it was over, and I was going to do it. But as I laid there I thought about my sister, my friends and my life. I thought of how everything would change and of everything I'd be leaving behind. I thought I'd at least give it another try since I'd be getting my phone back tomorrow. So I took the pills and snuck them back into their containers. Today when I look back, I'm actually happy I didn't do it. I just hope I can last till summer. If I can make it till then I can party whenever I want, make some bank, go to Panama with my friends, then get the hell out of this town and go to college. The girls and the parties are going to be unbelievable! I'll probably just smoke and drink whatever I can get my hands on until then just to pass the time. I can't wait to be around people like me! IU is all I have ever dreamed of. Maybe this place and these people are just what are causing my depression. I can't wait to leave. To live my own life. Now that makes me smile. I still look at the time in between with hatred though. I'll just be the craziest mother fucker around for a while. I'm thinking about just trying every drug ever. Sounds like a hell of a time.

<u>January 24</u>

Pretty boring last two days. It's hard to ever be positive in this life. Parents still being very constrictive. I CAN NOT WAIT TO GET OUT OF THIS TOWN.

I've really been struggling. High school girls are a fucking joke. One of my friends from the hospital had a really rough night tonight and almost had to go back. If you can hear me … …, I love you. It is not your time baby girl. I'm almost tearing up now. I wish someone could understand the pain I go through. I'm heart-sick. I bought my own cigs for the first time today. The days are passing by so slooow. I have to have something to get me through it, and they help calm me down.

January 25

Do you think it's sad that I'm scared to listen to the voicemail my dad left me? Heck, I'm scared to talk to my parents at all. Anyways, I slept in today I was so tired and worn out. I went to see my ex. She deserves a second chance. It went well. My parents only let me stay like an hour and a half. It was nice to get back in the bedroom even though we had to be quiet. I never cum inside her even with protection and her being on the pill. I just can't do that to her. Or myself. I didn't smoke anything today so that's a plus. Getting back with her would definitely help me stay clean, but I don't know what I want yet. It's so hard to stay clean after you've started doing drugs. Another day's gone by. My best friend got accepted to … … yesterday. That's only an hour from where I'll be. I'm going to start going to baseball soon. It should be a pretty fun and good season. I have senioritis really bad as far as school goes. Never doing any work or studying. Pretty tired. Not going to call my dad back. Uh-oh.

I want to start writing and making music again. It is one of my favorite things to do. Our high school play director got mad at me for "wasting my talent." I would do it if I didn't have sports. Me and my friends are still trying to finish our first album. It's just for fun. … … keeps telling me I must do American Idol. I might try it someday.

I'm worried about … …. I hate not being able to do anything to help. I want to help.

I toughened up and called my dad back. It went well! He is coming to see me and my sister tomorrow. I guess I'm finally doing this thing right.

<u>January 26</u>

Just watched the Hoosiers piss away another game. Awesome. Our girls lost tonight too. Unbelievable. I'm tired of watching all the teams I like suck ass. I've been pretty pissed off most of the day. I chain smoked earlier to relieve myself. I saw my dad. He was as stingy and rude as ever. Worst part is I got the news I can't play Church League basketball anymore because it's "not fair" according to the queef who runs it. Only got to play one game. 27 points in the twenty minutes I got to play. … … backed out on his word that I could play just because some pussy on another team went and cried about it to him. Some rich prick that wants his team to be the best. He let down me, my friends and my family. I'm going anyway. They're going to have to drag me out of there. How can you take basketball away from a kid that lost his season because he had to be hospitalized? That's just the kind of bullshit I've been talking about. A lot of my friends are being assholes too. I'm just not going to talk anymore. Here we go again. FUCKING DEPRESSION.

January 27

I've tried my best to get along with my parents, but I am FUCKING TIRED OF IT! I'm tired of being scared to come home because I'm afraid I'll get screamed at or hit. I'm tired of never being able to do anything I want. I've been a perfect little kid lately right? So I asked my parents if I could do two different things with my friends tonight. And guess what I got!? A NO TO BOTH OF THEM! And a rude I'LL SEE YOU AT HOME from the mother! Fuck you. Horrible parents.

You are the only problems in my life. You have failed. Fuck you. I am so pissed. You know what? I'm going to fucking take it. I'm going to sacrifice myself for everyone else out there. So people will learn what is right. I am giving myself to the world, its people, and everything else out there. Please learn from me. I want to help. I'm going to start by carving a cross into my chest/stomach.

I can't explain the pain. Keith just came in and exploded on me. Screamed as loud as he could. Took everything I had again. I heard them talking about how they're done with me. I have nowhere to go and no way to get there. I might just walk forever. I don't know what's going to happen to me tonight. I don't know what to do. I can't explain the pain. The hurt. The dread. I can't even write right. The pain. My chest is aching. My heart is sick with pain. Pain. Pain.

Pain. Pain. Pain. Pain. Pain. Pain. Pain. Pain. Suffering. Suffering. Suffering. Torture. Torture. Torture. Scared. Hurt. Hurt. Betrayed. They hate me. They don't want me. They want me dead. They hate me. They don't want me. They want me dead. They hate me. They don't want me. They want me dead. They hate me. They don't want me. They want me dead. They hate me. They hate me. They wish I wasn't here. Never born. They gave up. I am so weak. I'm scared. They torture me. I'm shaking with hurt and fear. Help me. Help me. Help me please. PLEASE! I don't know what is going to happen. I have to go. I can hear them coming.

January 29

16 mg's of Ativan. 3250 mg's of Trazedone. You probably don't know what that means. It means I tried. It means I should be dead. My mom found me on my bed with the empty bottles. She

rushed me to the ER. I was gone for almost a day. When I woke up I couldn't walk, talk, move, see, hear, think, feel. I peed my hospital bed twice. I don't remember much from yesterday. I was in and out, but when I was awake I wasn't really there. I woke up this morning with an IV still in my arm and five heart monitors scattering around my chest. I haven't eaten much at all. I've been tired all day. They moved me to a different area with the rest of the loonies now that I can function. I got to talk to Uncle Joel, Matt and Will. It was great. I'm still on bad terms with my family. I have horrible memories from two nights ago. I don't really want to talk about it right now. I took every pill I could find. I'm lucky to be here. I'm going to start trying to work things out with my parents. I'm tired of making everyone cry. This hospital sucks. Totally boring. I'm the youngest in here. I'm stuck in the lowest of lows. I wish I could just be better.

January 30

Attempting suicide is a whole new ball game. There is an absolute line between life and death. Once you do it, there IS NO turning back. It's over. Period. My senses still aren't back to normal. I don't feel right. I'm happy I'm still here. Still sick with depression and tiredness. Hopefully my friends will come and visit me later. I made a list for my parents of the people I'd like to see. I hate this. I'm bored and antsy as hell.

My next step is just trying to beat all this. I don't know how. I can't stay positive or even happy. I'm so depressed. At least I've been clean for two days now. Woohoo! I'm sure staying off drugs is the only way to maintain a steady, positive life. If I can find happiness within myself, then time won't be able to take it away so easily. I know it has to happen inside of me. Inside of my heart. I have to find my place. I'm trying to get there. Just working out the kinks. I can't wait to get out of here and live the life I want. The good, Christian, happy, positive, helpful, hard-working, and so on kind of life. Not the hellacious one. I hope there will be more to tell.

My fucking parents found my fucking journal and fucking read all of it. Bullshit! I've never been more pissed off in my life. I'm going to fucking kill somebody. Mother fuckers! I'm flipping shit right now. They crossed the fucking line. I want to fucking kill. Dammit! FUCKING DAMMIT! It was my life. Fuck you! DAMMIT SHIT. LEAVE ME THE FUCK ALONE NOW! Fuck you!

I've never been so angry in my life. They're going to think a lot differently of me now. It's not fair that they did that to me. It was my life.

January 31

Now that I've been in here for a while I've really been able to organize my thoughts. I've had to stop being stubborn and admit that there is a problem here that needs to be fixed. I've learned and gained a lot of knowledge and strength with everything I've been through. Now that I've seen death, I truly understand life. I'm going to spend the next few days figuring out what I need to do with myself from this point.

I'm anxious about my family meeting today. If it goes well, so will my future. And vice-versa.

February 1

My family meeting went great yesterday. We've

developed a compromise that will last me till I can get out of this town. They also put my journal back where they found it. I'm getting 100% clean now. Thank you GOD and Jesus for getting me through this. My parents really did care.

My parents and doctors want me to stay in the hospital a little longer because they don't think I'm safe yet. I can understand that. I'm so antsy to get out of here. My nerves are tingling, and I can't settle down.

I got new information on the white powder. Apparently it wasn't crack either, but this stuff called bath salts. The doctor said it's the worst drug someone can do right now. Great. They said it can completely change people even if you only do it once. I guess it's a new, very dangerous drug. Apparently it's making people go crazy and even causing people to die. At least I'm past it and okay. I have to go to a hospital in Newburgh later so they figure me out. Wish me luck. I hope I'm not ruined.

I'm starting to feel normal again for the first time since my o.d. It's taken five days to even start to feel okay. I'm still restless and have the jitters pretty bad.

I've been moved to … … in Newburgh for better treatment. I got more information on bath salts. The nurse here said it was like meth. I'm glad I stopped when I did and never went back. They said I'm very lucky. They don't even know how lucky I really am though. I've recently been informed that when I cut my stomach up there was a very high chance for me to get seriously infected. I guess I better start living right before I stop getting lucky.

I can't stop moving around. I'm just pacing everywhere. This urge in my body is never satisfied. It's frieking horrible.

I'm so lonely. So confused. I just want to go home.

I miss my friends.

I miss my family.

I am horrified with myself. What if I permanently damaged my brain? Or my body? I can't believe I was in that bad of a state to do that. I could be dead. It is so not worth it. Not for a second. The pain it causes after the fact is hell. It still tries to draw me in. I will never cross that line again. I will always have control of me. There is too much good in this world for me to let myself be hampered by the isolate life of drugs. My family knows about everything I did now. That's why I got moved here for help. I'm ready for them to find out the extent of the damage I've done to myself so I can stop worrying about it all day and night.

I'm crying my eyes out. Homesick.

<u>February 2</u>

I beat the sun out of bed today, did a little exercising and ate breakfast. Makes me feel a lot better in the morning. That is when I can actually get the motivation to get up, which isn't too often.

The first night is over now so I'm not as homesick anymore. I really wish I could see my friends though. And my sister. Anyways, today we start fixing my problems. Yay!!!!

My greatest fear has been confirmed. The drug I did was in fact bath salts. There is little known about the drug, but I'm learning as much as I can. It's the white powder that continues to haunt me. They are saying it's kind of a mix between cocaine and meth, as far as its high and addictiveness. I can't believe I had withdraws from using for just a couple of days. I can still feel its urge inside of me, begging me to do it again. It is very toxic, and they are still unsure about what it has done to my body and mind. I'm glad I was cut off when I was, and I'm clean now, and I still feel like Elliott.

My body is still getting over the overdose. I'm still extremely anxious and shaky. I can't ever remember if what happens is a dream or if I'm awake. This is even worse than coming off the bath salts. I remember lying on the couch in the fetal position in my mom's lap and screaming for two strait days. But with this my mind and body won't stop moving. The days are endless and miserable.

Pretty good day so far. Good group sessions. I'm really bored so I write a lot. Only bad part right now is finding out all the horrors of bath salts. I'm scared. I feel so horrible about it. I should be seeing the doctor soon.

I just want to go home.

Doc finally came to see me. I'm getting blood work done soon. He's putting me on a mood stabilizer because of the bipolar swings I've been experiencing. It should help with the anger, mood, anxiety, emotion and depression swings. He told me I can be diagnosed with bipolar disorder, manic depression, major depression and borderline personality disorder. PTSD is there too. But he says I'm too young for him to feel comfortable actually diagnosing me with all of them at once. Lucky me. At least I know there's a reason behind the madness that has been going on. I sure hope this stuff works. Extremely tired.

I just love tossing and turning at night. You know what I love even more? The 50 mg's of Trazedone they give me for sleep. Really? Cause it took an hour for over 3000 mg's to knock me out just last week. I really can't wait to get home. This was the longest day of my life. But since I can't sleep or even lay still, I might as well write. I hate nights. They give all my thoughts a chance to run together and torture me until I finally fall asleep. I'm so restless it sucks. I was able to relax a total of zero minutes today. Tis not very much. I've been thinking about Matt a lot lately. My cousin and best friend. He came and saw me at ... . He told me about how when he found out what I did, he just sat down on his bed and cried. I've never seen him cry. I wish I could take away all the pain I'm causing other people and put it on myself. I don't even care anymore. My feelings are completely stunted anyway. I can barely feel any emotion at all anymore. I'm so tired I can't think to write, but I can't quiet my mind to sleep. I hate this.

I've been trying piece together the night of my attempt. I feel like you deserve to know what happened. So this is what I can remember, from the moment I left you, to whenever I started writing again... I went into my parents' bedroom and took all the Ativan I could find from their hiding place that I already knew out about. I took the whole bottle and went and hid it in my room. Then I went to the bathroom and brought back my whole bottle of Trazedone. Back in my room I laid out all the pills on my bed. Then I went back to the bathroom and filled up a cup of water. I went back to my room and made the decision to take to take the Ativan first so I wouldn't be able to feel anything after too long because I wanted to carve a cross into my chest. I wouldn't end up conscience enough to do that though. I took about two or three at a time with the water until they were gone. There were 16 of them. Then I moved to the Trazedone. There 32 ½ of them. One by one I took every one of them till they were gone too. I took the picture of Jesus off my wall and held it against my chest while I laid there in the dark and soaked up the feeling. I heard my mom crying downstairs so I immediately jumped up and ran down to her because the sound broke my heart. I tried to console her because Keith had just walked out on us. As I tried to care for her she started blaming everything on me. So I went back upstairs and laid down again. I just stared at the ceiling for half a hour. That's when she came upstairs. I could hear her looking around in the bathroom. I remember hoping she wouldn't discover the bottles were missing, but soon she came to my room and asked me if I knew where my Trazedone was. I told her no. Then I could hear her frantically searching the whole upstairs for it. She finally came back in and sternly asked me, Elliott where is your Trazedone bottle!? So I took my right arm and flopped it over towards the pillows I had hid the bottles under. She walked over to them, stared at the empty bottles and asked me where all the pills were. At that point I kind of tapped on my stomach and said, “In me.” She said okay, come with me. She took me to the bathroom and tried to make me throw up, but I couldn’t do it. So she told my sister we had to go to the hospital and there we went. Aubrey had been shut in her room for most of it. She got left there alone with no idea what was going on except that mom was taking me to the hospital. She was there by herself. No way to talk to anyone or figure out anything that was going on. I had no idea then the pain I had caused her. My mom rushed us to the emergency room. She told them I had over-dosed. They sat me in a wheelchair and asked me what I had taken. After I told them, they said I was very lucky, rushed me to the ICU, laid me on a bed, put the air in my nose, stuck the IV into my left arm and put the heartbeat monitors on my chest. That’s the last thing I remember until about a day later when my eyes opened. All I saw were streaks of light. Just yellow, green and blue lines going every direction. I couldn't talk. I couldn't hear, smell, feel, any of it. I was numb. I didn't have any of my senses. I couldn't move. I kept coming in and out of consciousness. All did when I was awake was hallucinate. I couldn't think. I had no idea what was going on. Then I peed the bed. They had to undress me and change all my sheets with me still lying there in it. I couldn't do anything about it or help them at all. I just laid there incapable. My parents got to see everything. Literally. The nurse put a sheet over me to cover my wet, crippled, naked body. Later in the night, as I laid there dazing in and out, trying to move and speak, I did it again. So they had to clean me a second time. Then I got to go for a "walk." Assisted by the nurse and my father, I clumsily clambered down the hallway as if I was trying to defeat a Japanese obstacle course. I spent another night in critical care. The next day I woke up, and they moved me to the behavioral unit. I finally had to consciously lie there and think about how I had failed and given up. And all the people I had hurt and devastated. I thought about my dad, who had to receive a phone call from an hour away about how his only son had attempted to kill himself and was in critical care. My mom, who found and saved me after I had done it. My sister, who was upstairs with me and could hear me doing it. My step-dad, who had left the house because of my actions. My grandparents, who had to receive calls all around the country about what I had done, and there was nothing they could do. My cousins, my friends, my sisters, my family. Everyone who I had let down. And I was still alive. I was lucky, and they still had to go through the pain. When I finally came to 100%, 5 or 6 days later, I cried and didn't stop. I couldn't believe myself. I felt even worse than I did before. I wanted to see everyone and comfort them and apologize for what I had done. When I finally did see them for the first time it was horrifying. I lost it. I wept uncontrollably. My heart was torn apart time and again. Please listen to me when I tell you it is not worth it. It is not the only solution to your problems. There is an answer. Trust me. I've seen every side of this. Don't fool yourself. Don't do it to yourself. Don't do it to them. It does get better. You've just got to keep battling through it. You can get there. There is another side you can reach. I know it seems like the pain will never end. But you can get through it. There is light. Be stronger than I was. You can hate me for what I did. I completely understand. But don't make the mistakes I made. Win your battle.

It feels like one of those nights when I was little. When I would have to come home from my dads on Sunday. I would lie in bed and see his face in my mind and feel so empty to know he was gone again. Back to his home miles away. Without me. No way to see him. I cried myself to sleep every time until I was twelve years old. Keith called me a baby because I woke him up crying, or I would have to go into their room to get my mom. Now it's that same feeling. I miss all of them.

February 3

One of the greatest achievements in life is being happy with what we are and what we have. If we waste our time desiring what we are not and what we are without, then we will fail in many aspects of our lives. Be driven to accomplish your dreams and ambitions, but be sure not to over-rate money. Money causes us to over-look life's most important gifts. Don't get caught up in a world not worth living. Let us make the most of our one chance.

I think everyone should attend a group therapy session at least once in their life. Everyone has some problems they'd like to vent about. But I'm really talking about the emotional outlet it provides for the heart. Listening to other people's stories is truly humbling. At a certain point you learn that you don't have to hold back your tears and pain anymore. Today … … spoke of her children and later talked about me to my surprise. She made my heart fill up with hope. I guess simply being outgoing to everyone pays off in the long run. It was all I could do to refrain from getting up and hugging her. Seeing others cry in the circle today was also refreshing. It made me feel a lot more secure with the group. I wish I could help them with their problems. Everyone has something to share. I really believe in trying it at least once. It really helps you find yourself, and that is one of the hardest things for anyone to do. I am so thankful for all I have been given and everything that has happened to me. I wouldn't change it for anything in the world. I feel so blessed. I really do.

Today marks three weeks with no drugs or alcohol! Besides the o.d., that's just a whole different story. It's been over a week without a cigarette too, even though I'm very tempted. Staying positive.

I just cried because of my own story for the first time ever in group. I lost control because I realized all the pain I must be causing my little sister. I'm her biggest role model, and she has had to watch me go down a horrible path lately. I've let her down because of the things I've done, and I can not stand that. I feel so terrible about it.

It's hard to think about the fact that I'm lucky to be alive. It's hard to wrap my mind around. It just feels weird. It really makes me stop and think. Puts life in a whole, new, beautiful light.

As I sit here crying tears of happiness and thinking about all the wonderful things life has to offer, I can't help but look back at the last three months and smile. Even after all the horrible things that happened. The strength and knowledge I have gained is remarkable. You couldn't put a price tag on it. I'm so lucky to be here in so many ways. My family is great. My doctors are doing great. The people here at the hospital are awesome, and everyone is getting better. I love seeing everyone smiling. There is an itchy stitch in my heart full of joy and happiness right now. I'm leaving the life of hell behind. I've come out of this such a better person. I still wouldn't take any of it away for the world. I've gained a huge sense of love and understanding. I've met people who have changed my life. I can't wait to get started with my new life back home. A happy, peaceful, loving life. With everything I've learned, I plan to attack all the wrong in the world and change it for the better. I want to make a difference. I am emotionally cleansed. I am connected with the LORD. My past is past. I can not believe these tears of joy. These tears of victory over the fiercest battle. These tears that cleanse my soul for my new journey ahead. It is clear and beautiful. Life is beautiful. Feelings are good once again. I finally see why I'm here, and I finally feel worth again. Hope and worth. It means so much just to be able to feel happy again. For the first time in months, I'm ready to live.

February 4

I woke up feeling exceptional this morning! I'm making pretty good friends with someone on the unit named Curt. We have great open talks with each other, and we click pretty well. We are going to keep in touch after we leave.

I've never realized the wonders that compliments can pay. Curt told me after group that I'm half his age, and he's never been inspired by someone more than me. He just made my day, my week and my month. Before he told me, I had walked out of group because I'd gotten so irritated with someone's stupid ass stories. But Curt completely flipped my mood around. I went from huffing and puffing to smiling and proud of what I've worked so hard for. Never miss a chance you get to pay a compliment. The dividends it pays to the recipient are insurmountable. And on the other hand, resist the temptation to put others down. It usually has an even stronger effect expect in a negative way. Hurting people is so easy to do, and we usually don't even realize we're doing it. There is absolutely no need for it. Be true to yourself, and be the better person! You have the power to control what you say and what you do. And your actions can change people's mood, emotions, self esteem, and therefore, life. Make the right choice. How you affect others directly affects you. Putting people down will only make you feel worse in the end, when it really matters. Compliments pay off in great ways. For both parties. Trust me. I've been on both sides.

I've been thinking about expectations. The way the world is today - If you do something once, people will expect it from you every time after. And the more you do something, the more people will start to expect it of you in the future.

So I had to stop and ask myself ... What do I want people to expect of me? We need to sit ourselves down and really think and focus on this question. If we notice that we are doing things we don't want to be expected of, we must change for the better. If we notice ourselves doing things we do want be expected of, we must do these things even more. I need to be nicer and less tempered, especially when things don't go my way. That's my next goal in life. Let's keep growing. Together.

P.S. - I completely disapprove of people putting expectations on others. Expectations lead people in directions they don't want to go. They cause the expectee a lot of anger and the expected a lot of pain. I feel like we must be more respectful of others and let them do their thing. Expectations caused me to do things I hated, which in turn caused a lot of my depression. The only thing we should ever expect of others is that they be and stay true to themselves.

How do you want to be viewed by others? How do you want to view yourself? Stop. Take a moment. Really think about that.

I must learn to live without regrets. I've decided that they are about the dumbest thing ever. I can't change the past! All the horrible things that have happened to me have made me learn so much. The more you get through, the stronger you become. Always remember what you have done and gone through, but never regret it. It happened for a reason. There is nothing you can do about it now. The past is set in stone. You have to accept it and move forward. Learn from the mistakes you make, but don't dwell over them. The only way to get over something is to move on. You did what you did for a reason.

Just like forgiving others, you must learn to forgive yourself. When you look back and wish you would have done something different, just look forward and know that you will make the right decision next time. From making a mistake in a basketball game, to feeling like you didn't do enough with life, remember that in the end there are more important things. In the end what matters is that you were true to yourself and to the LORD. Remember who you are. Stay true to yourself and the things that are important to you.

I can honestly say I wouldn't take back my suicide attempt if I was offered the chance. It has put me through a life changing experience greater than I could ever imagine. I feel fortunate to be able to remember everything I had to go through. It makes my feelings of actual happiness so much sweeter, and it makes my life so much more worth it. Oddly enough, I've been thinking about my attempt a lot tonight. Mostly about how crazy the hallucinations were when I opened my eyes. At least I can tell myself that I'll never have to go through that again. A big improvement I need to make with myself is my irritability. I guess it did help me relax when my Hoosiers beat Purdue tonight. If they would just win all the time I would be fine. But that brings up a good point. Everything is easy when things are going our way, but how we handle the hard times is what defines us. I have to implement this to my every day life if I'm going to be a better person. Being here has given me so much hope. I really want to make a difference in the world during my life. People don't understand what they should about suicide and life. Plain and simple. And I think I can help. So I've made up my mind that I am dedicating my life to try my best to help the world with its understanding of such topics. It's hard stuff to talk about yes, but it can not be ignored. It's way too important to be over-looked like it has been. People's lives and life itself is being taken for granted way too much. I've talked to Curt about my plan, and he's been very supportive. I feel like the reason I'm still here is so I can do this. I truly believe that with all my heart.

February 5

Embrace your feelings. Let them flow through you. Feel them in your heart. Let them over-flow into your whole body. Focus all your energy on yourself. Let the outside world disappear for a moment. Hold on to your feelings. Allow yourself to be cleansed by the true you. Search inside yourself. You are searching for your identity. Who do you want to be? How do you want to live? What do you want from life? The time is now. Begin. The longer you wait, the harder it becomes to start. Let time be your friend. Don't let yourself waste away. You have to make the decision. You have to decide. This is no one else's but your own. Be brave. Be strong. Reach inside of you. Find you. Embrace you. Focus on you. Let you flourish. Allow you to come into the world. Know you are always safe inside yourself. Only you make the choices now. No one else can take it away. Become you. Be you. Release your beauty. You have control now.

I just experienced the most beautiful natural high from music therapy. Stunning. We all picked songs and listened to them and sang together. Beautiful. I'm actually shaking I've been so touched.

Curt continues to make my days here absolutely ten times more wonderful and worth it. He just called me his new little brother. This place has absolutely brought me to my knees.

Being in the hospital keeps making me relive the horrors of my past. From before I started writing. My world was so different. I thought I was actually living in hell. Ocd had taken me over. It caused horrible thoughts to stream through my head every single second of every single day. I couldn't control my own thoughts. It completely controlled me. I couldn't stop it. It was too strong. It even controlled my actions. My whole life was consumed by the compulsions. I had to satisfy it every second in order to move on to the next. But it never stopped. I only moved on to what the next obsession wanted. It made me into the absolute perfectionist I am. I couldn't live. Couldn't focus. It was like I was always gasping for air. I hated being awake because it was just ocd all day. And the next. And the next. And the next. And then it was too much. I began to hate life. The anxiety it caused me when I tried to fight it gave me anxiety attacks. I had one or more attack a day. I was forced to surrender to its power. Power it only had because I was so weak. I had so many compulsions I constantly had to do that I didn't even have a life anymore. There was never a second for me to be me. I was never happy. So I sought therapy for the first time. But before we could get anywhere the obsessions turned suicidal. All day and night. It's all I could think about. Plans to kill myself. It lied to me. Whispered how much easier things would be. How perfect it would be if all the pain could just stop in an instant. It became torturous. It kept growing and growing on its power. Every day felt like a month. In hell. Everything I did had to be perfect, but whatever I did was never good enough. Not only for others, but for myself. The perfectionism drove me mad. The obsessions brainwashed me. They told me I wasn't worthy enough to go to Heaven if I didn't do the compulsions. And that was all it took to over-take me, because Heaven was always the only real, important goal in my life. It scared me. I started asking for forgiveness aloud every time I felt like I'd sinned. For things as minor as cursing. I even apologized aloud if I had a bad thought. It was torture. People thought I was crazy. I barely slept. I didn't have time. When I did try to I just laid there with racing thoughts running circles in my head, competing against each other to see which one could make me scream the loudest throughout the night. I wasn't allowed to have an A-. I had to be completely flawless in everyone else's eyes. I never had any time for family or friends and especially myself. Ever. Soon I lost everything I had ever worked for and everyone I ever cared about. But that wasn't enough for it, no no no, it had to take me too. And eventually it did. I gave up. Its empire had risen to its peak. Elliott was gone. Lost somewhere deep within the shadows. Shadows that led him into inescapable darkness. To death's dark desire. But for some reason that he will never know, a light crept in. And the light was so Almighty that his black stricken eyes were opened. He was born again. A new man.

I just talked to someone here about a gang he's in. I tried as hard as I could to help him. After a while he finally admitted to me that he wants out of it. He was mostly concerned with the punishment he knows he'll receive if he leaves. Getting the shit beat out of him is the only way out. He said they'd do it bad enough that he'd be close to death, and then they'd just leave him there. The only advice I could give him was from an experience I once had when I had to approach a situation where I knew violence would be present. I told him about one time when I had really pissed someone off, and I knew the next time we met I was going to get my ass kicked. So all I did was went and found the guy, said I was unprotected, and told him that he could go ahead and do whatever he wanted to me. I just put my arms out to my sides and stared at him. And all he could do was stare back. He immediately lost all of his tension and anger. Then he just smiled at me and we talked it out. Like men. Today we are best friends. So that's why I told ... ... to never approach violence with violence. I hope he can make it through it. Sometimes we get ourselves into messes we can't handle, and we end having to suffer major consequences for our actions. Hopefully he can win this battle and leave all that stuff in his past. I really care about him and everyone here. It's like we are all bonded and in this together. I love it.

We had a spirituality group today since it's Sunday. It was incredible. I was so happy to finally rediscover my faith in GOD and Jesus and

The Bible and Christianity. I have such a strong love and importance for it all in my life. I know the best way for me to live the life I want all starts with the passion I have to be the best Christian I can be. Also, there are not words to describe how meaningful and beneficial praying is to me.

Ever since I started seeing life through a different light I've been daydreaming a lot about nature. I know it sounds weird, and it is definitely random, but I love to think about just leaving everything and living out in the beautiful, wondrous world. I think about the birds chirping in the cool breeze and the colorful, rustling leaves. I think about the little animals running around having the time of their lives. The green meadows touched only by sunlight. The streams of water trickling over the pebbles. The sounds of the invisibles orchestrating in the night. The little ponds. The mountains and the trees. And it's only me and the earth. There's no schedule to meet, no bills to pay, no worries to harm my way. I am connected with the world around me. It is a beautiful thought. Sends shivers down my spine and dimples to my face. A beautiful feeling. I love to just lie there and close my eyes and let nature take me over. Let my senses absorb the perfection around me. I often think that technology and advances in the world and inventions are the worst things that ever happened to us. How peaceful and happy life must have been way back when. It is an over-looked world. Vastly under-rated. I long for it like I now long for the terrible things in our world today. Maybe someday we can escape. Get out of this trap society has made for us and really, actually live. Live for ourselves and for each other and only for goodness. There is a chance. I just wish people could see. I am so inspired by Walden and other transcendentalist works. It makes sense. I dream of committing to and having all that someday. No more of the crap this world drops on us every day. Nature. It is inside all of us. If we just open up, let go and see. It is in our hearts. Nature. It is inside of me.

I got to meet Curt's family and best friend! I was so excited. I actually got to give them advice too. It felt great to help. I can tell Curt and I are going to be life long friends.

For some reason my mood dampened just a bit ago. I have learned how to control my mood better though. I just went and talked to Curt. He cheered me up more than any medicine ever could. Or recreational activity might I add. There's something far better about reaching good feelings through yourself rather using a drug or medicine to get there. It's so much more real and exhilarating and powerful. It's good to know I can deal with my problems in a healthy way now. What a life saver. I can honestly say Curt has done more for me in four days than most of my friends have in my whole life.

… … just called me her son. She is such a great woman. I am so blessed. Everything I've gone through is a huge blessing. To get me where I am today.

I can not believe the horrors I keep finding out about bath salts. It horrifies me. It makes me feel lucky, but at the same time it absolutely scares the shit out of me. I look back and remember when I was doing it, and it petrifies me. How am I still here? Still functioning normal? Still writing? I'm starting to shake again.

I've been thinking about …… a lot. Two months ago my plans were to spend the rest of my life with her. I was so deeply in love. She was closer to me than anyone else in the world. Besides maybe Matt. My whole heart was for her. Absolutely. And when she left me a few weeks ago I was so depressed, so at the bottom, that I couldn't even feel it. Not one bit. It didn't affect me at all. Yes I will always love her and care about her, we were together a long time and shared tons of great experiences, but I don't have any relationship feelings for her anymore. She hurt me too much when I needed her most. Now my heart is somewhere else. It's going to be hard telling her. I'm worried about her.

This world deserves peace. This world deserves an answer. Its people are beckoning for help … The answer is inside of us. Inside of each of our hearts. We all want the same thing. We all have the same dream. But we've been blinded. Blinded by today's society. So forget that for a moment. Forget everything and focus, it'll still be here when you get back. Take a moment. Look inside your heart. Find the truth. Find you. Find the happiness. The reason. Find where others stand to you. Take off society's blindfold that has built us into robots. Find yourself. Together we must stand. We are one people. Everyone is scared to venture into such a great task. I say we give it a shot. I believe we all want this. To come together. This world as a whole needs an intervention. Its people need to rise up. Be strong. Discover what life really means. Life is so much more. It defeats society in a heartbeat if you only give it the chance. The task is not easy. You have to absolutely believe it within yourself. Make the choice. Be the difference. Forget everything for a moment. Forget being tough. Forget being ignorant. Take down your guard. Just for a second. Dive into your heart. It's a beautiful place. Discover who you really are and what you truly believe. You'll find your answer in there. Hiding in the corner trying not be seen. Because that is what society has told it to do. Today's society doesn't want the true you to come out. So walk over to it. Embrace it. The past is done, over with, gone. It doesn't matter anymore. Embrace the answer you and I and everyone has been searching for, for such a long time. Each person has their own unique answer. I can't tell you what yours is, you must find it for yourself. But what I can tell you is that in the end, we are all the same. We all want the same things from life. Yet we are also different. Each of our answers is unique and only ours. The answers are there. And once they are combined, we achieve the ultimate victory. Together they are the most powerful thing anyone could ever imagine. More unbelievable than I can conceive. I have found myself. My answer. My purpose. My reason. My faith. If we will all just stop a moment and see, we will find it. The outcome we as a people can create together will turn this world into the answer you find for yourself. If you do your part, our world will be everything you ever needed. Everything you ever dreamed about. Everything you ever imagined. When Jesus returns it will be done on Earth as it is in Heaven. Don't just say the words, think about the prayer He taught us to pray. It is right there. Allow yourself to be delivered from evil. Do your best to defeat the temptation of sin. Allow the LORD to help you and guide you. It takes each and every one of us. No we can't make Earth into Heaven, but the more of us who live the Holy way, the better this world will become. The more GOD will be pleased with His people. It makes me smile to think about it. How lucky we are to have GOD and Jesus and Heaven all waiting. How blessed we are. Let us not spoil our chance to make a difference while we are here. Be a warrior of GOD. Find your answer.

Live it.

My Answer

Feeling. If there is one word that can describe why we do every single thing we do, it is feeling. Feelings. They control our actions. Every single thing we do, every single decision we make, is based off of how it will make us feel. Our feelings are what give evil its power. It is simple - we sin because it makes us feel good. Any sin you have ever committed, you did because you believed that that action would make you feel good. Whether at that moment, or in the future. You did it for your own best interests. Because that is how people are. It's all about me. It's all about how I can benefit myself. Whether it is alcohol, drugs, gambling, lying, cheating, murder, hate, judgment, theft, selfishness, violence, any of the seven deadliest, defying the Ten Commandments, any and every sin. Every time we sin is a time evil has overcome us. Evil = sin. Sin = selfishness. Selfishness is evil. We must be self<u>less</u>. Selflessness is where good comes from. We humans are so blinded! GOD has told us we will be better off when we do not sin! We will <u>feel</u> better if we do not sin! So whatever you are sinning for, in belief that it will make you feel good/better in a situation, if you do not commit the sin, you will end up in a much better state than if you would have. Even if it doesn't seem like it at that moment. So, say you lie to cover up something you did wrong and you end up getting off the hook un-penalized. At that time you feel good about how things turned out. And you say to yourself, ahh everyone sins and it benefited me so one time can't hurt. But in reality, things will actually turn out better for you if you tell the truth and accept the consequences. At the time you will probably think otherwise, but GOD has told us this is the way it is, so trust in the LORD and your faith will be rewarded. On the other hand, if you believe otherwise, then you believe you are above GOD. And if this is the case, then I am sorry for you, and I pray for you. I am sorry that unfortunate circumstances in your life have brought you to be in this state. For I can not imagine the punishment that awaits. But I can assure you that nothing earthly could ever compare to anything we experience after we leave. And it is not worth believing that our short lives here are more important than where we will spend eternity. The belief that committing the sin will in fact benefit us is the devil on our shoulder doing his best to blind us from the truth that is GOD. Sin is what causes the hurt and pain in the world. The devil's deception is the root of all evil. Be stronger than that. Be stronger than him. Every path has snakes, but we have a Guardian. There is a reason GOD is above in Heaven, and satan is below in hell. Think about it. GOD knows all. He already knows what decisions you will make.

He already knows where you will end. But He doesn't control it, you do. He created us and blessed us with free will. He didn't want a bunch of robots walking around that He controlled and did whatever He wanted with. There would be no point to that. He blessed us humans with a life of free will to do what we please and make our own decisions. And He blessed us with all the wonderful things on this earth. And He looks down and hopes to see us living right and living with Him in our lives, not evil. He has given us the chance to live the most beautiful lives we could ever imagine. We just have to follow His word. It is wrong to believe our lives can be better with disregard to Him. He has done all of this for us! He wants us to be happy! He will make things perfect for us if we just let Him! Stop eating from the forbidden tree. It is our choice! We just have to live according to His word and have faith. We have one obstacle. he is below. But we can do this! We have GOD

Almighty! King of Heaven and Earth! LORD! Rejoice! Whose team do you want to be on? Forever. Making the excuse that everyone sins so it is just okay to do whenever is just another thing satan is trying to deceive you about. We may not be able to be completely sin free, but GOD said all is possible through Him so I believe in doing our best at all times. The Bible is our guide to His word. It is GOD's rulebook of life for His people to follow. It is where we find the answers to everything we need to know concerning the LORD and life. Things were perfect before evil, and they will be after. What we see as betterment for ourselves as we commit sin is really not the case. Don't be selfish and take the easy road. Always have the big picture in mind. Only when we live with the big picture to guide us, may we truly be happy and fulfilled in each moment. Like I said, our actions are controlled by how we think we will feel as a result. So why not listen to the LORD, not commit the sin, and always come out of every situation feeling the best it is possible you can. If you think about it, if someone was to be completely selfless, they would never have a bad feeling. The only pain they would ever feel would be for others. Isn't that the whole reason we sin in the first place? To benefit for ourselves? To make ourselves feel good/better? If you are selfish and fall to evil, all you ever need is more and more to keep making you happy. But the selfless person is always happy. He doesn't require selfish action in order to help out his own feelings. He is always fulfilled. Sin is so backwards! Doing it defies its whole purpose to us! Its purpose is make things easier and better for us, but not doing it will always have greater benefits for us! So if you think about it, sinning is only for the foolish! Do not take the easy way out! You will always be fulfilled if you follow GOD's word and live a selfless life. The LORD has promised us Paradise. Defeat the temptation. Defeat evil. Defeat the devil. It is your choice which path you choose! he can't make you do anything! My goal is to be as selfless as I possibly can. I've realized it is not about me. Selflessness is my key. I will sin as little as I possibly can. And I will always be happy because of this! I will always have a smile on my face! I am so happy! Just from committing to this life and idea. If everyone did the same, we would all always be happy! Oh rejoice! You may say it is not possible. But if everyone joins in it can happen! I am so happy. I feel like I've fallen in loveee. And I will feel like this forever... Money has no meaning. As long as there may be food in my stomach, water in my mouth, breath in my lungs, and my LORD above, then I am living in my perfect world. Everything makes sense now. I'll never have to be scared, worried or angry. Love, joy, happiness and faith will always overflow through my heart and soul. I am complete with faith and truly connected with the LORD. I can be whoever I want to be. I am completely happy and fulfilled. In reality, by completely committing to a selfless life, I have actually given myself ultimate happiness. And I didn't even do it for me. Isn't it incredible how things work out that way? It is so simple. That is GOD for you. That is my answer.

February 6

I didn't get to sleep till after 3 last night because I was having such a great time. I had a great talk with Curt, and I was on such a happy streak I just wanted to hold on to it. Curt and I have really exciting plans for after we leave. I am so happy to be stable again. And happy.

P.S. - Curt only has half his face shaved because his electric razor quit working mid-shave. Hahaha. It's classic!

Just got a one on one request from another patient to be my room-mate. I'm glad he is seeking my guidance. It makes me feel well about what I've been doing. My answer was an immediate and absolute yes. He could have just walked in and crashed without asking, and he would have been 100% welcome. Any of the people here could. Anyone at all could.

I feel horrible. I'm so anxious I feel like throwing up.

I'm getting pretty nervous about leaving. I know it will be soon. It seems Curt will be leaving even sooner. I know I'll cry when he goes. I will feel very empty here without him. We know that we will continue our friendship outside of here, but I'm not going be used to him not always being right there for me when I need him. We made a bet over who can learn to play the guitar first after we get out. We are ready to move on with our new lives. I feel like I'm becoming a man. Like I'm entering a new stage of my life. I want to be a therapist. I love helping people. Especially people who are going through the things I've had to. My bipolar-coaster has finally returned to the tracks and is steady. Words can't describe how happy I am to be where I am now. When I get out I will begin a new set of challenges. I will take the next step in the miracle of a journey I have been on. I've come to realize that no matter what, no matter how much you live your life the right way, there will always be problems and obstacles that test every last bit of you. Now I know how to deal with these things. I can't run away, I must do the approaching. Don't forget me, especially in the hard times. You are forever in my heart and soul. But sadly, in the end it is like a mother releasing her young out into the wild. Once she teaches them all she knows, she must let go. I have given my heart to you and taught you everything I know. But when my stay here ends, so will we. I have to set you free into your own new journey. I know we will succeed, but it still hurts me to have to do this. We must part ways with a smile and an understanding that each of us has our own answer and direction we must follow. And no matter what, we will always have each other. We are moving on to better places. We must go with our heads held high. We must take our knowledge and apply it without wasting a second. There is nothing that could ever come between us. We shall take our paths and ride them into the abyss. Where do we want to end up? Think about it. Use the words I have given to you so that you may understand the pain, love and life I have been blessed with. It is a priceless feeling be able to look in the mirror and know that all is well. It brings peace and joy to my heart. I know that I am saved and that my Father is waiting above, in Paradise, in a presence more perfect than I can ever imagine.

Doc said my discharge will be soon. I went to my first AA meeting. They said I need it to help with my previous drug issues. I am finally starting the mood stabilizer tonight to help with my imbalance, depression and disorders.

GOD keeps throwing battles at us. Not out of anger, but because He loves us. He knows us. He is Almighty. It is our job to never quit. To never give up. To be strong in the moments we feel weak. He cares. He wants the most out of us. He lets us make our own decisions. He made us a promise. And in moments of pain and suffering we have to look up. When we cry we must look up. It is hard. It is trying. No one ever said we were going to walk through life and always have a smile on our face. We can not do it alone. We need our LORD. We need each other. Don't let your troubles take you away. Battle with me. Battle. With. Me. When you want to give up. When you are tired of trying. Drop to your knees. Raise your arms to the sky. And pray to the LORD above. Praise your GOD. Let it out. It is time to be strong. I know the hardest days of my life are ahead of me. And one of my closest friends is leaving tonight. You know what? I went and cried in my room when I found out. I felt the sky was falling again. That it was too hard. But I'm not giving up again! Listen to me! I'm not giving up again! You're going to have to hold me down and stop my heart before you see weakness in me again. I am going to win this! I am going to live this life like it's meant to be lived! GOD's hands have caught me. I have won. In the hardest moments I have become victorious. Because of what I've been through. Because of what I've seen. Because of what I've felt. Because of what I've learned. And because of everything I've told you. I have one Judge. I fear only Him. Everything I have told you is truth from my heart. I have learned everything does happen for a reason, and it is our job to deal with it the best we can. I don't ever have to worry again, because I know that whatever happens, it is all part of GOD's plan. I have finally proven to myself that I can win. That we can win. We can do it. Have faith. It is in all of us. It is. Find it.

February 7

People being cheerful and happy around me make me feel that way too. Formula: surround myself with people who are how I want to be. It applies for everything. I want to be around sober, determined, kind, outgoing, happy people because that's how I want to be. It rubs off on me. It's good for me.

One of the most important things I've learned through this whole experience is - You have to listen to other people's advice and knowledge if you want to get better. One of the hardest things for me to accept was that I don't know everything. I finally had to realize there are plenty of people and plenty of professionals out there who know how to get the job done. I had to get over my self-indulged ignorance. And now that I have, it is a great load off the shoulders.

Here are some quotes I've come up with that I have jotted down throughout my journal. I'm definitely going to share them with the world and use them in my life. There are also some things for some special women down there.

Do not forget where you have been, it is the

reason you are here.

How do you want to be remembered? Will you be missed or forgotten?

You can't change your past, but you can determine your future.

There is a time and a place for everything. Now is the time to live, and here is the place to do it.

The decisions we make affect everyone.

If you are looking for an excuse, a mirror is never too far away.

Allow others to learn from your example.

Control what you can control.

Actions speak louder than words, so shut up and do it.

Impossible is an opinion.

The more haters there are - the more scared people that are listening.

If you live with should've, would've and could've, you are lying to yourself, because the present is what it is.

Your feelings in about situation are relative to what you are used to and what you expect.

One must be willing to give before one may expect to receive.

Selfishness is ignorance.

There are two kinds of people in the world: People who put others before themselves and people who put themselves before others.

How would you describe the image in the mirror? ... Is that how others would describe it too?

The opinions you and the LORD have of you are the only ones that matter.

The best opportunities only come once.

Whatever it is, it is possible.

If you spend your time dreaming about everything you don't have, you will lose everything you do have.

There will be times you are scared, nervous and unconfident ... Remember who you are, how you got here, and who you are willing to be ... You are strong enough.

If this is your plan GOD, I trust you. No complaints, no doubts, no regrets.

Bittersweet Reality

I can not escape this fantasy. My mind is caught in the skies. I see her everywhere I go. The thought of her innocent touch is killing me. I can not carry on without her. She takes my breath away. Her presence stops time. Her beauty is the trigger to my heartbeat. It gives me life. Her body makes me shiver. My aching heart can not leave her behind. I wish she could know the truth. My love was born when I first saw her face. But she will never spare this poor man's soul. She feels not the wind and lightning I feel when we are near. She just pushes me aside. But my love will never die. The light will never leave my eye. So I'll just be here skipping stones and thinking that one day things will be right. Oh baby you've gotta see. You can't give up. So get out and do this for me. Anyone can see that nothing else really matters to me. You are my queen.

T.S.

The look in your eye draws me closer and closer. Your personality is brighter than the sun. Your smile melts me to the floor. But your beauty keeps my heart from stopping. It brings me back to life. Your unattainable, Heavenly beauty. You've a body that my emotions crave day and night. A touch that sparks passion throughout my soul. A voice that ignites a fire I can't control. It's the way you move. The way you look at me. Your presence defines me. My mind is addicted to you. Every breathe I take is searching for your love. A love I found not because of the traits above. But because of what's inside of you. The most precious heart I have ever known.

Heaven's Child

Oh how I love the girl. The way she makes me feel. Her precious lips on mine. Every kiss feels like the first. Her body so enticing. Her scent so inviting. Her laugh so exciting. Her gaze makes my heart come undone. It flutters like a middle school crush. Forever happy in her presence. When she's gone I feel like I'm underwater, scrambling for a surface I will never find. She is all I need. All I desire. She fulfills me. Seizes my emotions. The one I would run away with. Leave the world behind. Live happily till time is no more. In a place far from everything. Where all we have is each other. And that's all we need. My life, my love, my heart. Forever.

Leaving tomorrow! I'm definitely ready. I got the room-mate for this last night. The big bad boy cried during one of our talks. I'm so proud of him. I believe he actually wants to get on the right path now. Another friend I won't let go of. One more day.

<u>February 8</u>

Today's the day. The next step in my journey soon begins. I am ready. I leave here at 6:30.

The boy suffers. He is lost. His mind is clouded. Confusion sets in. He is alone. He loses everyone and everything. He does horrible things to himself. His body. His mind. He is in pain. His mind tortures him. He loses control. Depression. Anxiety. Fear. Carelessness. Helplessness. Worthlessness. Hopelessness. He gives up ... The boy is saved. He gets another chance. He figures things out. He finally understands life and himself. He recovers into a whole new person ... The man puts others before himself.

He puts his faith, his family, his country, his people and his world all before himself. He sees the big picture. He is loving. He is caring. He knows who he is, what he wants and who he wants to be. He is willing to do whatever it will take to get there. He is true to himself. He is true to others. He is strong, inside and out. He respects everyone. He goes out of his way for strangers and friends alike. He is kind. He is always learning. Always humble. He leaves his hate and ignorance behind. Personable. Loyal. Trustworthy. Happy. Knowledgeable. Brave. Understanding. Accepting. Helpful. Lively. Eager … The man has found himself. He wins his battles. He has changed … The warrior knows that his toughest battles are ahead. That he will suffer again. That he will start to fall and lose his way. But the warrior is strong now. He is ready. He uses and pursues his strengths. He recognizes he is blessed with what he has been given. He can admit his faults. He accepts his weaknesses and works to make them his most reliable attributes. The warrior uses his past to overcome the present. He awaits his future with confidence. And the warrior is forever victorious. For hc is a warrior of GOD.

Life isn't going to hand itself to you. Life isn't going to be easy. It's not going to cuddle up in your lap and smile at you. It's going to test you. Your strength. Your weaknesses. And we have to battle in these instances. Many of us have become a weak people. Many of us don't have to work for or appreciate anything. And America is the worst right now. We expect everything to be handed to us. We have to learn. We have to learn that this life thing is a blessing. It's not something to just toss away and take for granted. It doesn't deserve a who cares attitude. It's our one and only chance here. And I believe it deserves a little respect for that. So of course the problem becomes dealing with the hard times. We have to become warriors in our own battles. We've got to fight. We can't give up. We can't let our problems and hard times control us and take us over. We have to decide how we want to live. That is our decision. We were given free will. And we are blessed to be in a country that freely allows us to make these decisions for ourselves. It's time to stop taking these kinds of things for granted. It's time to start seeing what life is all about. Because like I've said, we are only here once. Then we are gone. Forever. We will never be here again after this one life is over. We don't know when it's going end. One chance. One opportunity. One life. Ever. And right now is our time. So when these hard times come we have to realize that we are strong enough to get through them. We will do whatever it takes. We will fight to the end. We won't give up. We will stand our ground. And we will make the right decisions for the right reasons. Because we are warriors. I've become a warrior through my pain and suffering and the battles that I've won. But you don't have to go through all that to be a warrior. Each of us has problems and challenges we face every single day. And depending on how we deal with these problems is what defines us as weak or strong. As victims or as warriors. We have to be courageous and brave when life is putting us down the most. When evil is on our shoulder tempting us to do something that we know isn't right, we must be strong willed and do the right thing. That is when we have to reach deep down inside of us to come through. It takes our hearts and our minds. It takes our inner beliefs and our inner strengths we have developed. We have to know what we want to live for so that when things are worst, we can rely on our emotional instincts to get us through. We have to prepare ourselves. I've learned that taking the easy way out and giving up is never the answer. Believe me when I say, you will get through it. The pain will stop. The more you have to go through, the stronger you will become. The more you have to go through, the more GOD believes in you, in your strength, in your will power. Now, are you going to let it take you over and roll over and say this is too hard and it's not worth it? Or are you going to make the decision for yourself that you are going to win these battles? That you too are going to be a warrior? And that you are going to be yourself and a person of GOD? Are you going to execute your values or someone else's? Are you are going to find the true you in your heart and let it out into the world? It is each of our decisions. How do you want to do this? Are you just going to take the easy road and go through the motions like everyone else does? Or are you actually going to do something!? Are you going to live!? Let's go! It's a matter of self respect. And a lot of us have lost that. All we care about is being accepted by society. We just roll over when it gets too hard.

We give up, we stop caring. But that is not the answer my friend. I am blessed to have found mine. I want to help people. I want to help the world. Once you find yourself and become a warrior, the rewards have no end. Trust me, it is the most beautiful and fulfilling thing you could ever imagine. I am a completely different person with a completely different outlook on life. I love the person I have become. It took some tragic events for me to get here, and I want to teach people what I've learned so we all don't have to go through that pain to get here. We have to be warriors. We have to stand strong. Imagine how good you will feel if you step up in the hard times, and win your toughest battles. Imagine the satisfaction and the happiness that will flow through your heart. Compare that to how you will feel if you give up. The horrible, low feeling you get if you just quit. The more you win, the greater the rewards get. As you continue to overcome, your enemies and problems keep growing weaker and weaker. You've just got to find yourself. You've got to block everything else out, and focus on your heart. You have to find what it is you stand for and be strong and brave enough to release it out into the world. You only have one chance to do it! You are unique! You can do it! You have control over yourself, no one else does. Be a warrior. Be strong. There's no more need for weakness. You are better than that now. Those days are over. Your new journey can begin at any moment. You just have to let it. Do not procrastinate anymore! It only gets harder the longer you wait. Give it a chance! Start living! Stop yourself for a moment, block out everything else and make the decision. Do it for yourself. Soon it'll start to rub off on others around you. You will love the outcome. It may take a while for you to realize it, but if you stay true to yourself, there is no way you won't come out a happier and better person. So, in conclusion, search inside yourself and discover who you really are. No more excuses. Life is too short. Put your true self out into the world. Be a warrior. The hard times will come, and you will want to give up. But you can defeat them. You will win. Don't be afraid. Winning battles will put a true smile on your face. You will be happy with yourself and who you have become. From there you will find your love in the people around you and where you want them to fit into your life. It happens in your heart. We all love that warm, tingly sensation our heart sends out when we are happy and excited. So go get it! You are not being selfish by looking out for your own well being. Once you find yourself, you will soon find the true meaning of others in your life. And that is a remarkable feeling. Do it for yourself, and do it for them. Take a deep breath and smile. Love life! You are worth it! Do not give up. That my friend, is not worth it.

As I've seen my life pass before my eyes in the past few days, I've started to realize many things. I have discovered a different view of life I had never thought about before. We are born. We have our own bodies. Our own brains. Our own wills. We are completely ourselves. We are supremely lucky to be living as we are. We get to think our own thoughts, have our own feelings and perform our own actions. But what is the point of life? I mean it could literally end at any moment. Why has society made us view life in such a structured, pre-planned way? In reality we are all ourselves. We all have our own insides, our own feelings and aspirations. We have been given this one life. We have one chance to live here on Earth and then, in one single, unforeseen moment, it is all over. At any second it could be over. Each breath we take could be our last. So we must savor each moment and live it like it is our last. We must make the most of what we have been given. We must do everything our hearts lead us to while we continue to remain living people in God's world. We must always live in a way that is true to ourselves. We should do what we want, what makes us happy. We mustn't dwell in the past or the future because all we have is right now. Every second should be spent fulfilling the you that is you and only you. We have one life, we have to live it! Now! From now till the day we die. We have to find ourselves and live accordingly. We don't have to do what society expects and demands of us. All that matters is how YOU FEEL. Life is measured by the perfect moments. The ones that will last forever. So stop living someone else's plan for you. It is never too late. It is never too soon. Live for yourself. Live for GOD. Enjoy every second of YOUR life that YOU have HERE. Forget money. Forget society's expectations. If you are doing things the way you want and you love your life then society has no power. Love yourself. Love your time. It is a gift. Every breath is. Love what YOU WANT to. You were born for you. Live with meaning and purpose. Be with the people you want to be with and the people who make you happy. Make them a part of your life, love them and enjoy your life with them in it. For me, I want to help others deal with the struggles of life. I want to have a wife and kids. I want to work to live and live to work. By helping people. And when I'm not, I want to be with my family in nature, on a beach somewhere, whatever and wherever we want. I understand that I only get to do this once. Regrets are for the ignorant and the weak. All we truly have is ourselves. Soon it will be gone. FOREVER. And I will live to make sure I spend my forever in Heaven, in Paradise, with GOD and Jesus. Never ending time. Not here. But there. Where things are perfect. Forever. It truly is my biggest goal in life. Too often people get blinded by everyday life and society for all the wrong reasons. Life is like a test. Don't overlook it. Take a moment and think about forever. And how you would like to spend it. Dedicate yourself to your way of living. I live to serve GOD. Through GOD I am myself, and I live to be me. I am blessed, and I wish to help others see they are too. Real happiness lies within each of our hearts. Find yours. Nothing else matters. LIVE. Stop stressing. Stop worrying. Smile! You're alive! You are you. I'm smiling. I love life right now. Every second. That's how it should be. In one word ... JOY.

P.S. - I wish some beautiful lady would see it this way too and just run away with me! Haha.

It's been a very long, tough road. Life's not easy. Through it all I've become a very understanding person. Understanding that people do what they do for reasons. Reasons that pertain to problems in their own lives. That everyone has problems of their own. I have learned that whatever is going on in someone's life plays the biggest role in their actions. That the worse someone is, the more help they need. Not hate. Not enemies. But friends, love and support. There would be no such thing as good if there wasn't bad. I've learned to accept other people's unkindness towards me with love. If they are being hateful, then there is something going on in their life that is causing them to be that way. They are being that way because of some problem inside of them, inside of their life, their mind and their heart. Anything in the world could be happening with them. Their actions are caused by something that's going on with them that only they understand. Retorting back gets us nowhere. It only increases both parties' side of the problem. We must accept people for who they are and respect what they are going through. We must do right for them. I am having to change a lot about myself so I can get better at this. With the more people who get better, the better this world will become. Although perfection can never be achieved, we can sure as hell do our best to get as close as we can. I've been thinking about what other people must think of me, and how their judgments are very wrong and unfair. They don't know my story. They don't know what I've been through. They don't understand me. So it made me think about how I judge other people, and I realized that I don't know any of those things about them either. I myself was an arrogant, selfish, prick before. It made me feel better about myself. Now I've learned to be a better person, and I've made the decision to never judge again. No one. No matter what. From the smallest of things to the largest. Whether it's the clothes they wear, the words they say or their actions. Not bullies, not liars. Not cheaters, not thieves. Not terrorists, not rapists. No one. There's a saying - You would never judge someone if you knew their story. And that is absolutely true. Yes what they are doing may appear to be the most heinous or horrible thing you could ever imagine. But haven't you ever wondered to yourself ... how could someone ever do something like that? And you could never come up with an answer? Well the reason you can't figure out the answer is because you are not them! It is as simple as that! They know why they did it, and they did it for a reason. Of course there has to be justice for crimes against the law. But beyond that it is between the person and GOD. I'll let Him do the real punishing. And as for me, I automatically forgive them. Because something is going on that is causing them to do it. What if they're messed up in the head? What if they can't put food on the table for their family? What if they are being threatened? What if they were tortured at a young age? They are dealing with something horrible in their life that is causing their actions. Like bullies for example. Everyone knows that bullies only do the things they do because of their own problems and insecurities. I have nothing against anyone anymore. And also, it's not my right to judge others. The only true Judge is above. Everything happens for a reason. They do what they do for a reason. You don't know what goes on in their head. You don't know their life, what they've gone through, what they're going through. Only they know the truth. And chances are, if you're the one judging, you've probably got it a lot better off than them in the first place. So instead of hating them for it, we should try to help them and pray for them. To them what they did seemed like the right, or the only thing to do. They made their decision based on something else going on with them. I respect everyone now. I love everyone. We are all equal in His eyes. So we are in mine too. We only know about ourselves, not about them. This world can not achieve great things with all the selfishness that is present. After we have found ourselves, we must learn to think about and help others more. Because we all need it! We must forget our differences, accept each other and come together. No judging. I feel so much better inside since releasing all the hate in my heart. I do expect people to do the right thing, but I must forgive when they don't. I accept that my parents are the way they are for a reason. And now that my head is clear, I see why they did the things they did. They were always trying their best to help. They love and care about me more than I've ever deserved, and they are the greatest parents I could ever ask for. I accept that my coach is the way he is because he believes that that is how it is done best. I accept everything and everyone now. There is no reason for hate or anger. It feels great to have realized this. I am full of love and care. No one is perfect. That was Jesus. I'm striving to be as much like Him as I possibly can. I love life.

People aren't going to like you. People aren't going to accept you. They're going to try to bring you down. You're going to be tempted to go back to your old ways. Your head will become so clouded that you will block out all the good that has happened to you, and you will focus only on the bad that you are experiencing at that moment. This is a very hard thing to deal with, for we all want to be accepted. But if you can learn to catch yourself, and instead block out the negative, you will take another step in becoming a warrior. You will realize that you are, in fact, accepted. And by a better group of people. Anyone who tries to bring you down or change you for the worse is not a good person. They are a person that evil has overcome. Be a person of GOD. You will be strong enough to deal with such circumstances if you believe in yourself and what you are doing. Challenge yourself. Be stronger than the temptations. You know you want to win, sometimes our minds just get lazy. Be a champion of life. Overcome. You can do it. It's your life. It's your decision.

I am chemically imbalanced. I am obsessive compulsive. I am bipolar. I am severe major depressive. I am manic depressive. I am borderline personality. I am post traumatic stress. I am happy. I am blessed. I am saved. I am strong. I am here. I am ready. I am true. I am me.

I give myself to Him. Because He gave me life. And everything I have. He saved my life. He saved my soul. He gave me a second chance. I live for Him now. Like I always should have. I understand now. He blessed me. He loves me. And I love Him with all my heart. I owe my life to Him. I have to stop feeling guilty and regretting everything I did in the past. He is the one Judge. He forgives if we have faith and ask to be forgiven. I forgive because He forgives. I must forgive myself and move on because He has blessed me and given me the opportunity. I have to accept the gift He has given me. The gift of life and Jesus and forgiveness. Jesus who came to the world as GOD's son. Who died for our sins. Who died so we may be forgiven. So we may join Him in everlasting Paradise. We take it all for granted. We don't even appreciate it. Well those days are over for me. It is disrespectful to the LORD for me to be anything but as much like Jesus Christ as I possibly can. Jesus, GOD on Earth. I strive to be as much like Him as I can. Every second of every day. To give like He does. To love like He does. And to see everyone as equals because that is how He made us and how He views us. It is foolish to think otherwise. It is foolish to believe anything different than what He has spoken because He is the Creator and He is the LORD. It is foolish for me to think anything I may do or gain here is more important than anything that is GOD and that is above. I now expect nothing less of myself than to be the best Christian that it is possible for me to be. I have been so blinded by society and what others think, so caught up in every day life. But that stuff doesn't even compare to the real importance of life, and what life is really all about. I thank my LORD every day for what He has done for me, us and the world. He is within me. Inside of my heart. All of my negative thoughts and feelings and emotions are gone. The hate. The anger. The sloth, gluttony, lust, ignorance, frustration, envy, pride, lies, wrath, meanness and greed. I am refilled with hope. With faith. With love. With happiness, understanding, care, peace, forgiveness, truth, spirit and joy. I mustn't dishonor Him and dwell on what is past and waste everything He has done for me. I am so blessed and so fortunate. I give myself to Him. I dedicate my life to helping others see His way too. I allow Him to come into this world through me. I must view life and the world through his eyes. I am letting Him inside of me and releasing His word and His unconditional love out into the world. I love Him with all my heart. I can not wait for the day when I may join Him in Heaven forever. He had given us everything. The greatest gift of all. Paradise awaits. I beckon for His presence. As for while I am here, I give my life to helping His people, in hope that others may find their faith in Him as well.

You are a magnificent person. You have so much beauty inside of you that is ready to burst out into the world. You have feelings and emotions that are ready to spring out of your heart. The world is yours. Allow it to embrace you. Let it come inside. Let your soul radiate out of you into its welcoming arms. Free the you that is inside.

Allow it to carry you along on its glorious journey.

Well brother, I am home. It truly is a great feeling. Tomorrow I begin outpatient therapy with the hospital. I'll be doing that for about a month. Curt will be there! It hurts me to have to end our journey together, but it is a necessary step in our moving forward. I've really enjoyed writing this journal. It will always have a very special place in my heart and life. Curt says the world should hear what I have to say. I don't know about that, but my future is dedicated to helping others. It is my love and my passion. In final thoughts I just want to say good luck. Remember everything we've been through. Good and bad. Remember my words. Don't be shy to do what is right. Don't be weak. Those days are over. Be yourself, stay true, be strong, make a difference. We will win this battle.

Together. So live life right. Have faith in the LORD above. And lastly, do not ever give up. EVER.

CPSIA information can be obtained
at www.ICGtesting.com
Printed in the USA
LVHW022018020120
642351LV00014B/1138